CW01619987

Traditional Cumbrian Cooking with Mrs Simkins

Published in Great Britain in 2025 by Dalesman Publishing
The Gatehouse, Skipton Castle, Skipton BD23 1AL

www.dalesman.co.uk

This book must not be circulated in any form of binding or cover other than that in which it is published and without similar condition of this being imposed on the subsequent purchaser. No part of this publication may be reproduced, stored on a retrieval system or transmitted in any form, or by any means, electronic, mechanical, photocopying, recording or otherwise, without either prior permission in writing from the publisher or a licence permitting restricted copying.

In the United Kingdom such licences are issued by the Copyright Licensing Agency, Third Floor, 6 Hays Lane, London SE1 2HB.

The right of Mrs Simkins is identified as author of this work has been asserted in accordance with Copyright Designs and Patents Acts 1988.

All reasonable care has been taken to ensure the accuracy of the recipes and instructions in this book. However, any liability for inaccuracies or errors relating to the material contained within this book is expressly fully excluded of the law.

During cooking, you may not always achieve the desired results. Oven temperatures vary between different appliances, and different equipment may affect the desired outcome. All measurements are approximate. Neither Dalesman Publishing Limited nor Mrs Simkins accept any responsibility or liability for the end results of the recipes included in this book.

© Mrs Simkins 2025

All recipe photographs are the author's own.

ISBN: 978-185568-411-9

Printed in China for 1010 Printing UK Ltd

All rights reserved.

ACKNOWLEDGEMENTS

- *Recipes of Lakeland*, compiled by readers of *Cumbria* magazine, The Dalesman Publishing Company Ltd, 1966 and 1982 editions
- *Lakeland Cookery*, compiled from recipes supplied by readers of *Cumbria* magazine
- The Dalesman Publishing Company Ltd, 1975
- *Old Northern Recipes*, Joan Poulson, Hendon Publishing Co Ltd, 1975
- *Lakeland Recipes Old & New*, Joan Poulson, Countryside Publications Ltd, 1978
- *Traditional North-Country Recipes*, Joan Poulson, 1984, Cicerone Press
- The Foods of England website: www.foodsofengland.co.uk

Many thanks to all the readers of *Cumbria* magazine, old and new, who have sent in family recipes from Cumbria in days gone by. Keep them coming!

Mrs Simkins

INTRODUCTION

Here is a collection of traditional Cumbrian recipes, based on notes made by Cumbrian families, going back generations.

Not many records of these examples of home cooking exist nowadays, but happily I had plenty of the genuine article to consult from *Cumbria* magazine readers' recipe archives.

The old recipes have been given a bit of a makeover to suit modern tastes and kitchens, and they feature the simple, homely ingredients typical of the old counties of Cumberland, Westmorland and the Furness region of Lancashire, which together became the newly established county of Cumbria in the 1970s.

Oats grow well in the northern climate and were utilised frequently in the Lake District, along with lamb from the sheep on the fells, fish from the lakes, including the now comparatively rare Arctic char, and of course the exotic dried fruits, brown sugar and potent rum and spices that arrived in the ports of Whitehaven, Workington and Maryport in the 1700s — all of which have characterised Cumbrian cooking ever since. Lakeland locals were among the first in the country to try these new goods from afar.

The food of Lakeland was often hearty, suitable for hardworking people with outdoor occupations, with lots of home baking to treat the family and tempt the tourists who first started arriving in the region in the seventeenth and eighteenth centuries.

Now read on and see which recipes you fancy trying first…

Mrs Simkins

CONTENTS

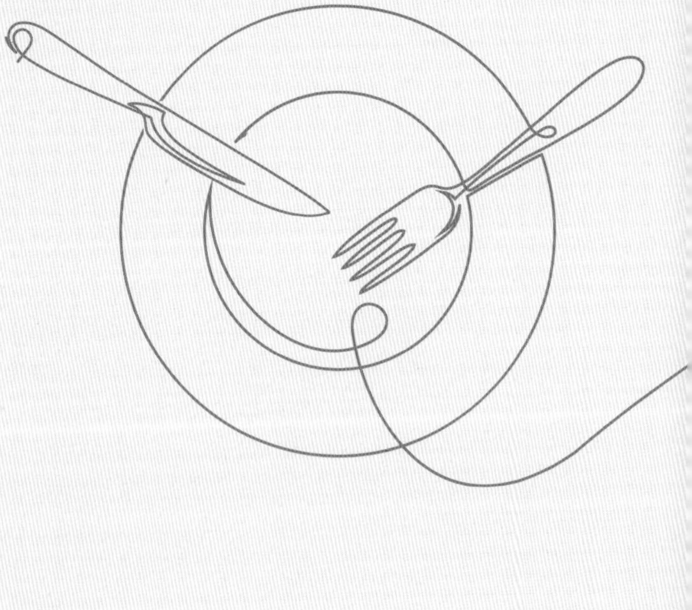

Savoury

CARROTS IN SWEET HAZELNUT SAUCE

SERVES 4-6, AS A SIDE DISH

Born on July 28, 1866, Beatrix Potter fell in love with the Lake District and made it her adopted home. She became a respected sheep farmer and, using the profits from her famous children's books, helped save the Herdwick sheep from extinction.

Her well-known animal characters loved their vegetables, herbs, nuts, fruits and honey. If Peter Rabbit had ever invited his friend Squirrel Nutkin round for dinner, this carrot recipe, cooked with hazelnuts and honey, would have been perfect!

- 450g young carrots, scrubbed or lightly peeled
- 2 level teaspoons butter
- Cold water to cover

For the sauce

- 25g plain flour
- 25g softened butter
- 75g ground hazelnuts, see note below
- 300ml milk
- 1 teaspoon runny honey, or to taste
- Pinch sea salt, or to taste
- Finely chopped parsley to finish

- Slice the carrots into dainty rounds about ½cm thick. Cook them in the butter with water to cover; bring to the boil, then simmer gently until just tender. Lift out the carrots and keep them warm
- Meanwhile, work the flour gradually into the butter until you have a thick paste. Grind the hazelnuts
- Add the milk to the remaining liquid in the carrot pan and drop in pieces of the butter and flour paste. Heat to almost boiling, whisking constantly with a balloon whisk until thickened
- Once thickened, whisk in the ground hazelnuts. Add the honey and salt to taste, whisking thoroughly. Add a drop more milk if it seems too thick. Return the carrots to the pan and heat through. Scatter with parsley to serve

NOTE

The practice of using ground nuts in soups and sauces dates back to medieval times. The technique of dropping pieces of paste, made from blending equal parts of flour and butter to thicken sauces, is known as *beurre manié* in French cuisine.

The sauce also works beautifully with other vegetables, broccoli and green beans in particular.

This recipe is based on an inventive one from a young housewife who lived in Silloth many years ago and was recorded by Joan Poulson and published in 1978 in *Lakeland Recipes Old & New*.

HAZELNUTS

You may be able to find ready ground hazelnuts in some shops, but otherwise use whole blanched ones and grind them in a coffee grinder or similar: you are aiming for the texture of ground almonds. Failing that, substitute with ground almonds.

CUMBERLAND HOT POT

SERVES 4

Not unlike the Westmorland tatie pot, this hearty dish is made with beef and, of course, the traditional black pudding that graces all the best Lakeland hotpots. You'll need floury potatoes to soak up all the gravy and juices. Serve with a green vegetable, mustard and pickled red cabbage.

- 450g shin of beef (or braising steak) trimmed and cut into bite-sized pieces
- 2 tablespoons oil
- 2 large carrots, sliced or cut into diagonal chunks
- 600ml cold water
- 1 large onion, sliced
- 2 rounded tablespoons flour
- 1 beef gel stock pot (or similar)
- 2 tablespoons malt vinegar (or use balsamic or red wine vinegar)
- Plenty of freshly ground black and ground white pepper
- Good grating of nutmeg
- Large pinch dried thyme
- 125-150g well-seasoned black pudding, not too fatty, thinly sliced
- 900g potatoes, very thinly sliced

Plus

- Butter for greasing and dotting

- Preheat fan oven to 150°C (170°C non-fan, gas mark 3 or equivalent). You will need a greased, lidded casserole dish
- Brown the beef in oil. Remove from the pan and keep warm
- Boil the carrots until tender in the measured amount of water. Reserve the cooking water
- Fry the onion in the oil until soft and golden. Add the flour and stir, then cook for a couple of minutes over a moderate heat, stirring frequently
- Stir in the carrot water and remaining water from the measured amount. Bring to the boil, still stirring
- Once smooth, stir in the stock pot, vinegar, pepper, nutmeg and thyme. Add the meat and carrots. Simmer for 3-5 minutes
- Starting and finishing with potatoes, layer the potatoes thickly in the dish, with the beef and gravy mix and the black pudding slices
- Cover and bake for 2 hours. Remove the lid, dot the top potato layer with butter and return to the oven for a further 20 minutes or until the potatoes are golden

CUMBERLAND OLD MUTTON SAUCER PIE

SERVES 4

Lakeland's own much-loved Herdwick sheep is a must for this flavoursome, traditional pie, adapted from an old recipe from Cockermouth.

Traditionally reared and grazed for centuries on grass and heather up on the fells, succulent Herdwick has a flavour like no other lamb, hogget or mutton. Shoulder and leg joints are fantastic roasted and served with Cumberland sauce; other cuts such as neck fillet, trimmed and diced shoulder, leg and chump are wonderful for stews, casseroles and pies. Saucer pies were once a popular standby in the Lakes: baked in saucers or small shallow dishes, they needed only a short time in the oven.

- 400g Herdwick mutton, hogget or lamb, trimmed and finely chopped
- 2 tablespoons oil
- 1 medium onion, peeled and diced
- 3-4 medium mushrooms, finely chopped
- 1 level tablespoon flour
- 2 tablespoons balsamic vinegar (or use malt vinegar)
- ½ vegetable gel stock pot (or favourite vegetable stock cube)
- 150ml hot water
- Leaves stripped from 2-3 sprigs of thyme
- 1-2 sprigs finely chopped parsley
- Freshly ground black and ground white pepper
- Light grating of nutmeg

Plus

- 220g plain flour
- 110g cold salted butter, diced
- 3 tablespoons cold water
- 1 small egg, beaten with a teaspoon of water

- Preheat fan oven to 190°C (210°C non-fan, gas mark 6 or equivalent)
- You will need a greased 22cm pie plate or 2 x 12cm pie dishes and a baking tray
- Fry the meat slowly until browning. Set aside and keep warm. Fry the onion slowly until soft, add the mushrooms and continue cooking until the onion turns golden and the mushrooms are soft
- Turn up the heat slightly and stir in the flour until it is all absorbed. Cook for a minute or two, stirring frequently. Stir in the vinegar until bubbling, add the gel stock pot and water. Stir until smooth and add the herbs and spices
- Continue to cook on a low heat until the gravy has thickened. Leave to cool
- Whiz the flour and butter into crumbs and add the water. Whiz until large crumbs form, remove from the processor and press gently into a smooth ball. Divide in 2, one piece slightly larger than the other. Roll the larger piece into a circle to line the dish and the smaller into a circle for the lid. Chill for 20-30 minutes if possible
- Spoon the filling into the dish, brush the rim with egg wash and position the lid. Trim the overhang and indent the edges with a vegetable peeler handle or similar. Brush with egg wash. Sit the dish on a tray and bake for 25 minutes or until golden brown

CUMBRIAN CHICKEN

SERVES 4

Here's a lovely old Cumbrian chicken recipe, ideal to come home to if you are having an active weekend out and about on the fells. You can pop it in a slow oven for the afternoon, or better still, a slow cooker. It also reheats beautifully if you have leftovers or want to prepare it the day before.

Serve with a baked or mashed potato and a green vegetable; pickled red cabbage and a dab of mustard wouldn't go amiss either.

TIP
The original recipe added a layer of sliced tomatoes to the top, so you can try that if you like.

- Approximately 1kg chicken, either a whole one, jointed, or a mix of boned thighs and breasts, or use all breasts if you prefer
- 2 tablespoons oil initially, plus 1-2 more for the roux
- 110g bacon, diced
- 1 large onion, halved and fairly thickly sliced
- 110g mushrooms, sliced
- 2 tablespoons plain flour
- 750ml hot chicken stock
- Black and white pepper, to taste
- Good pinch of dried thyme
- Fresh parsley, to serve

- Preheat fan oven to 150°C (170°C non-fan, gas mark 3 or equivalent)
- Heat 2 tablespoons of the oil and brown the chicken pieces on all sides
- Fry the bacon, onions and mushrooms
- Arrange the chicken, bacon and vegetables in the casserole dish
- Add a little more oil to the hot fat left in the pan and allow it to heat, stir in the flour a little at a time, making sure it is all amalgamated, and cook for a couple of minutes or so. Slowly and gradually stir in the hot stock, changing to a whisk as the mixture slackens
- Season with pepper, add the thyme, pour over the meat and vegetables in the dish, and cook for 1-2 hours in the oven or 3-4 hours on the medium setting of the slow cooker
- Sprinkle with chopped parsley before serving

FAIRY TOASTS

SERVES 2-4

Just the thing for an autumnal light lunch or supper, the original recipe for this delicious and substantial toasty snack appeared in *Recipes of Lakeland*, a collection from *Cumbria* magazine readers, published in 1966. Fairy very likely refers to fairy rings: the dainty rings of wild mushrooms that appear in grassland in September.

This slight variation includes garlic, and that warmly aromatic favourite Lakeland spice, mace. Parsley adds the finishing touch.

- 40g butter
- 1 tablespoon oil
- 250g mushrooms, sliced
- 1 garlic clove, finely chopped (or a squeeze of garlic purée)
- 25g plain flour
- 300ml milk
- Freshly ground black, ground white and cayenne pepper, to taste
- ¼ teaspoon ground mace
- A little salt, to taste
- 4 slices of bread
- 50g mature cheddar cheese, grated
- 3-4 small sprigs parsley, finely chopped

- Melt the butter in a lidded pan, add the oil and cook the mushrooms slowly, until soft but not brown. Add the garlic for the last 3-4 minutes of cooking time
- Sprinkle the flour over the mushrooms and stir in well. Cook for 3 minutes, stirring frequently, over a medium heat. Gradually add the milk, a little at a time, stirring constantly. Season with the different peppers, mace and salt
- Once the sauce is smooth, turn up the heat a little and simmer until thick, stirring constantly
- Meanwhile, toast the bread lightly on both sides
- Pile the mushroom mixture evenly on top of each slice (you won't need butter), spreading it out to the edges. Scatter thickly with the cheese and grill until the cheese is bubbling
- Sprinkle with chopped parsley and serve immediately

FARM CHEESE PATTIES

MAKES 18

This is based on an original Cumbrian farmhouse recipe collected by renowned cookery writer Joan Poulson back in the 1970s, and it was a very old recipe then.

Easy to make from simple ingredients, including dry bread, these little patties are absolutely delicious, ideal to eat at any time as a light snack or a meal, or to include in a picnic.

The original recipe specified mild cheese, but a mature cheddar works beautifully. It also called for ¼ pint of cream and ½ oz of melted butter, but plain milk works perfectly and is much less heavy and rich. There is also a note from Joan, mentioning a little grated onion as a good addition that's well worth trying.

For the pastry

- 180g plain flour
- 90g cold salted butter, diced
- 3 tablespoons cold water

For the filling

- 2 small-medium eggs, beaten
- 150ml pint milk
- 25g stale breadcrumbs (not too fine and powdery)
- 225g mature cheddar cheese, grated
- ¼ teaspoon dry mustard
- Cayenne, black and white pepper, to taste

- Preheat fan oven to 180°C (200°C non-fan, gas mark 6 or equivalent)
- You will need a 7cm cutter
- Make the pastry in the usual way or whiz up in a food processor: whiz the flour and butter into crumbs first, add the water and whiz until large clumps form
- Remove from the machine, form gently into a ball and flatten into a disc
- Chill in the fridge for 20-30 minutes then roll out a fraction thinner than a pound coin
- Cut out 18 circles and transfer them to the tart tin. Firm them in place very gently
- Whisk the eggs and add the milk, breadcrumbs, cheese and seasoning. Allow to stand for 30 minutes and divide between the pastry cases
- Bake for about 15 minutes or until the filling is puffed and golden

FISH PIE

SERVES 4

Fish is the traditional fare on Good Friday and this simple fish pie would be perfect. With its beautiful lakes and coast, fish has always been on the menu in Cumbria and there are several readers' fish pie recipes in *Cumbria* magazine's archives. Some are topped with pastry, one with a savoury crumble, but potato topped ones have always been a favourite.

Here's a potato one not unlike some of those recipes. Soothing and comforting, a lovely fish pie is always welcome.

- 1kg potatoes, boiled and mashed, with a little milk and pepper to taste
- 3 medium eggs, ideally at room temperature
- 600g cod or haddock (400g white fish and 200g smoked is a nice balance of flavours, but all white is fine)
- 300ml milk
- 3 level tablespoons cornflour
- ¼ teaspoon mustard powder and black, white and cayenne pepper to taste
- 2-3 sprigs parsley, finely chopped
- 50g grated cheddar cheese

- Preheat fan oven to 180°C (200°C non-fan, gas mark 6 or equivalent)
- You will need a greased ovenproof dish and a balloon whisk
- Lower the eggs carefully into boiling water and boil for 7 minutes. Remove from the heat immediately and plunge into cold water. Shell and set aside
- Lay the fish in a wide pan and pour over just enough cold water to cover
- With the pan lid on, bring to a simmer and poach the fish until it loses its translucency and becomes opaque: usually about 6-10 minutes. Set aside
- Mix the cornflour and seasoning to a smooth paste with a wooden spoon in a heavy-bottomed pan, with 2-3 tablespoons of milk from the measured amount. Gradually add the remaining milk: change to the whisk and whisk constantly
- Bring to the boil, still whisking. Lower the heat and whisk until smooth (if it seems a little stiff, you can add some of the fish cooking liquor, but not too much). Stir in the chopped parsley
- Flake the fish and quarter the eggs, then arrange in the dish. Pour the sauce over
- Cover with the mashed potato, smoothing it round the edges of the dish so the sauce won't bubble through. Make raised lines or wavy patterns with a fork and scatter with the grated cheese. Alternatively, dot with butter instead of cheese
- Bake in the oven for 30-35 minutes until piping hot and nicely browned on top. Serve with peas or a green salad

GAMMON AND APRICOT PIE

SERVES 2

Here's an adaptation of a lovely old recipe. Warm and comforting, yet beautifully light, either use leftover ham joint or gammon steak in this novel and tasty pie.

This serves two people as a light snack, or four with crusty bread and dark green vegetables, such as steamed savoy cabbage or curly kale.

- Approximately 450g (2lbs) cold, boiled potatoes
- 1 medium onion, diced
- 1 tablespoon oil or meat drippings
- 200-250g cold ham (or unsmoked gammon steak) cut into small cubes
- 10 soft-eating dried apricots, chopped
- ½ vegetable gel stock pot or similar
- Plenty of freshly ground black and ground white pepper
- 2 tablespoons hot water
- 2 tablespoons crème fraîche
- Knob of butter

- Preheat fan oven to 180°C (200°C non-fan, gas mark 6 or equivalent)
- You will need a 23cm pie plate or similar shallow baking dish
- Dice the equivalent of two small-medium potatoes and slice the rest. Keep separate
- Cook the onion slowly in the oil or dripping. If using gammon steak, add to the pan at this point
- If using leftover ham, wait and add with the apricots about 5 minutes before the onions are soft
- Stir in the ½ gel stock pot until dissolved. Season generously with pepper and add the hot water and crème fraîche. Stir and add the cubed potatoes. Cook gently for a further 5 minutes
- Pour the filling into the dish and arrange the sliced potatoes on top. Dot with butter and bake for 30-35 minutes until the potatoes are golden

HERB OR DOCK PUDDING

MAKES 1 LITRE PUDDING PLUS 2 MINI CAKES, OR 10 INDIVIDUAL CAKES

Puddings made from any kind of tender, young spring greenery, together with cereals that grow well in the north like barley and oatmeal, have been popular for aeons in northern counties. Emerging shoots and leaves were eagerly foraged after a winter of dry, preserved foods. Young nettles, dandelion, new shoots of bistort or sweet dock, aka Easter ledges, spring cabbage, parsley, spinach, Brussels sprouts tops, even young blackcurrant leaves, can all be used.

Steam as a pudding or shape into cakes and fry on both sides until golden for breakfast. The fried cakes in particular are very tasty and worth making often: savoury and good, as it used to say on jars of Marmite!

This recipe is similar to a young Lakeland housewife's recipe of many years ago from just outside Millom. She made it occasionally in the spring, as did her grandmother before her. She would serve the pudding with the Sunday roast, or for high tea with bacon. Any leftovers would be sliced and fried.

- 110g pearl barley, rinsed
- 450ml vegetable stock
- 1 medium onion, diced
- 5-6 spring onions, sliced
- 1-2 tablespoons oil and a teaspoon of butter
- 200g mixed spring leaves, washed and chopped (see above)
- 110g oatmeal
- 1 rounded tablespoon flour
- 1 large egg, beaten
- Ground white and freshly ground black pepper

- Preheat fan oven to 160°C (180°C non-fan, gas mark 4 or equivalent)
- Bring the barley to the boil in the stock. Simmer for 30 minutes or until soft
- Fry the onions slowly in the butter and oil until soft and sweet. Add the greens and wilt. Remove from the heat
- Add the barley, including the stock, to the pan. Stir in the oatmeal, flour, egg and pepper

For the pudding

- Transfer to a 1.1 litre pudding basin, the bottom lined with a circle of greaseproof paper
- Smooth level. Cover with double thickness greaseproof paper, pleated to allow for expansion. Tie with string and steam in the usual way, or stand in a roasting tin containing 2-3cm of warm water and bake for 40 minutes or until pale golden on top

For the cakes

- Shape the mixture into cakes and shallow fry in hot oil or bacon fat on both sides for 5-10 minutes until piping hot and golden. Serve with fried eggs and/or bacon

PEASE PUDDING FROM BRAMPTON

SERVES 8 OR MORE

Pease pottage, aka pease pudding, is one of our most ancient dishes. Still a big favourite in the north of England, for some reason it's rarely made down south. This version is based on a traditional recipe from Brampton, just east of Carlisle, and you can't get much further north than that!

Rather than simply pepper and salt, original pease puddings were often flavoured with more exotic ingredients, such as saffron, nutmeg and cinnamon. The Brampton pudding includes nutmeg and it makes all the difference.

If you prefer, reheat the mixture gently in a clean pan and serve as pottage without progressing to the egg stage. It's tasty, but the eggs give it an even more wonderful flavour, lighter texture and deeper colour. Both versions work brilliantly with sausages, ham or bacon, and a fried egg wouldn't go amiss either. It's also good in a bap or on toast.

Leftovers of either version can be reheated on the hob, in the microwave for a minute or two or sliced and fried.

- 500g split yellow peas, soaked overnight in cold water
- 1 medium-large onion, peeled and diced
- 25g butter, plus extra for dotting
- Freshly ground black pepper, ground white pepper and salt to taste
- Good grinding of nutmeg
- 2 medium eggs

- Preheat fan oven to 180°C (200°C non-fan, gas mark 6 or equivalent)
- Drain the peas, rinse and tip into a roomy pan with fresh water to cover
- Add onion and bring to the boil. Reduce to a gentle simmer and continue to cook for about 2 hours, until the peas are soft and the water has been absorbed
- Whiz in a food processor or blender with the butter, pepper, salt and nutmeg, until smooth but still slightly textured
- Alternatively, beat with a wooden spoon until smooth
- Next, beat in two well-whisked eggs, turn into a buttered dish, grate over more nutmeg, dot with butter and bake for 20 minutes in a preheated oven, until golden
- Both pottage and pudding will keep in the fridge for two or three days. Reheat until piping hot

PORK AND APPLE PASTIES

MAKES 2

What could be nicer than a golden brown, home-baked pasty as the autumn leaves start to fall? And here's a lovely one based on a reader's recipe from the *Cumbria* magazine archives. Eat hot with vegetables and gravy or cold with a salad.

- 200g strong bread flour (perfect for pasty pastry)
- 100g cold butter, diced (or use half butter and half lard or block vegetable shortening)
- ½ teaspoon salt
- 4 tablespoons cold water

Plus

- Approximately 300g lean pork, finely diced
- Salt to taste
- 2 good pinches of dried sage (optional)
- Freshly ground black pepper and ground white pepper
- 2 rounded (but not heaped) tablespoons of cold apple sauce (see method for recipe)
- Beaten egg to glaze

- You will need a baking tray lined with greaseproof paper
- Preheat fan oven to 160°C (180°C non-fan, gas mark 4 or equivalent)
- Put the fats, flour and salt into the bowl of a food processor and whiz into crumbs. Add the water and whiz into large clumps. Knead gently into a ball on a floured board
- Divide the pastry in two and form into two balls. Roll out into circles with a thickness of about ½cm
- Lay the circles on the baking tray. Spread the pork in the middle of each pasty, keeping it more to the lower middle, season with salt, sage (if using) and plenty of both peppers and spoon the apple sauce evenly on top. Brush the edges of the pastry with water
- Fold over the pastry and gently press the edges together as you go: crimp with your thumb and forefinger, first indenting with the side of your thumb and then pressing the pastry together as you go round
- Brush with beaten egg for a glossy, professional finish and bake, unpierced, for 50 minutes or until golden brown and the meat is cooked through

Apple Sauce

- This is sufficient for four, as it's difficult to make a smaller amount; leftovers are lovely with porridge, muesli or granola for breakfast
- Peel, core and slice three large Bramley apples into a saucepan, squeezing a little lemon juice over the slices as you cut them. Add 2-3 tablespoons of golden granulated sugar and 1-2 tablespoons of apple juice or water. Simmer on the hob until the apples are completely soft. Beat briskly with a wooden spoon into a rough purée with a little texture

POTTED CUMBERLAND HAM WITH ROSEMARY

SERVES 6-8

This tasty treat is based on an old Westmorland recipe. It's a handy idea for just after Christmas when there's still plenty of leftover Christmas ham, but it works well at any time of year. Use Cumberland ham, if available.

Delicious on toast, oatcakes, crackers or in sandwiches, it works beautifully with a dab of damson chutney or relish on the side.

The original recipe instructs you to mince the ham twice. If you don't have a mincer, use a food processor and pulse instead, but don't over-process as you need to retain some texture.

Make sure all equipment is scrupulously clean before you start, and you can easily halve ingredient quantities if you wish to make a smaller serving.

- 300g cooked ham, minced
- 50g unsalted butter, softened
- 6-12 rosemary needles, washed in hot water and rubbed dry, chopped very finely
- Freshly ground black pepper and grated nutmeg to taste

To finish

- Small sprig of rosemary to garnish, washed as before
- Clarified butter (see method)

- Combine the minced or pulsed ham in a roomy bowl with the butter, pepper, nutmeg and chopped rosemary. Beat with a wooden spoon until smooth or whiz carefully in a processor, making sure to retain some texture
- Pack into clean glass jars, check for air pockets and pour clarified butter over the top to seal. Garnish with rosemary and chill. Stores for up to 48 hours in the fridge

Clarified butter

- Cut 225g unsalted butter into small pieces
- Heat gently in a heavy-bottomed saucepan over a low heat until it spits, crackles and bubbles
- Remove the pan from the heat. Carefully skim the froth off the top with a tablespoon
- Pour through a sieve lined with clean muslin, or a disposable kitchen cloth, into a clean lidded jar, avoiding any of the solids collected on the bottom of the pan

TIP

You'll have plenty leftover, and clarified butter is excellent for frying. Normal butter burns easily: the solids are the part that burns, but once they are removed, you can cook with the butter on a higher heat and for longer without catching.

POTATO SOUP

SERVES 4

Homemade soup has always been a favourite in these parts. Here's one you don't see very often: a simple potato soup.

Traditional Lakeland potato soup recipes tend to contain milk, and maybe a spot of cream for a treat, which is lovely, but this equally creamy variation is made without either, just a little butter and oil.

Blending everything at the end is the secret to velvety smoothness.

- 1 tablespoon each butter and oil (use all oil if you prefer)
- 1 medium onion, diced
- 6-8 spring onions, sliced, or more to taste
- 1 vegetable gel stock pot or similar
- Freshly ground black and ground white pepper
- 4 medium-sized floury maincrop potatoes, weighing about 1kg in total
- Snipped chives or 2-3 lightly fried, sliced spring onions

- Fry the onion slowly and gently until soft and golden. Add the spring onions halfway through the cooking time
- Melt the gel stock pot into the onions and season with black and white pepper
- Meanwhile, peel the potatoes, cut into even-sized chunks, add cold water to cover and boil until the potatoes are tender
- Drain, retaining the cooking water, and mash: there's no need to add extra butter or milk
- Combine the onions and potatoes. Add some of the cooking water and whiz in a blender: you may need to do this in batches. Add more cooking liquid as needed
- Take care not to over-blend. Do just enough until the mixture is smooth, or you could turn it gloopy and gluey in texture
- Transfer to a pan and heat through until piping hot: try to avoid boiling as this can impair the flavour. Adjust seasoning if necessary
- Serve with crusty bread and garnish with snipped chives or some lightly fried, sliced spring onions

RAREBIT TRIPLE DECKER

SERVES 1-2

Who doesn't love Welsh rarebit? Here's a lovely three-layered toasted sandwich version based on an entry tucked away in *Recipes of Lakeland*, a compilation of *Cumbria* magazine readers' recipes published in 1966.

No one could say Welsh rarebit is specific to Cumbria, but this recipe was sent in as a reader's favourite all those years ago and is an especially nostalgic 1960s version, garnished with bacon rolls.

The rarebit seasoning wasn't specified, apart from the mustard powder and additional seasoning to taste, so I've used my own rarebit mix seasoning, plus an egg yolk for extra richness.

- 2 thin rashers of bacon (streaky works best and looks better, but use back if you prefer)
- 110g grated mature cheddar cheese
- 3 tablespoons milk
- Generous pinch of mustard powder (shop bought ready-made mustard is too salty)
- Good splash of Henderson's relish or Worcester sauce
- Dash of Tabasco or good shake of cayenne pepper
- Freshly ground black pepper to taste
- 1 medium egg yolk
- 3 slices of bread (white is recommended)
- Butter for spreading
- Tomato and cocktail onions to garnish, optional

- Fry the bacon rashers until cooked and turning golden but still pliable enough to roll
- Carefully remove the bacon from the pan, roll up each piece. Secure with cocktail sticks (cut into 2 smaller rolls, if you prefer). Keep warm
- Combine the cheese, milk, mustard and other seasoning in a pan and heat until melted. Stir in the egg yolk. Cook gently for another minute or two until the mixture thickens. Keep warm
- Toast the bread lightly
- Butter two slices on one side and spoon or spread the rarebit on the other side of both pieces
- Take the third slice and spoon or spread rarebit on both sides
- Lay one of the buttered slices, butter-side down, on your board or work surface, and lay the slice with rarebit on both sides on top
- Finish with the other buttered side, butter-side up, rarebit-side down, on top
- Transfer to the grill pan (preheat for best results). Lower the grill rack and give the rarebit stack a final toasting on each side until golden and you can see the filling is bubbling gently
- Cut in two triangles and top with the hot bacon rolls. Garnish with the cocktail onions and tomatoes, and serve immediately. A little salad is a nice accompaniment

SALMON SCOUSE

SERVES 4

Here's a handy recipe for Good Friday, tucked away in *Recipes of Lakeland*, a collection of recipes from *Cumbria* magazine readers, published in 1982. It's a simple mix of potatoes and salmon, but Arctic char may sometimes have been used years ago when it was more plentiful in the Lakes. Originally served with an egg sauce, parsley sauce is much more to modern tastes.

- Approximately 2-2.5kg of peeled potatoes, boiled, strained and smoothly mashed with butter, a little milk and black and white pepper to taste
- Approximately 400g poached or steamed fresh salmon, skin and bones removed, or the equivalent drained red or pink tinned salmon
- Butter and chopped parsley to finish

For the sauce

- 600ml milk
- 40g cornflour
- Freshly ground black, ground white and cayenne pepper, to taste
- ½ teaspoon mustard powder
- Salt to taste (optional)
- Knob of butter (optional)
- Handful of parsley, finely chopped

- Preheat fan oven to 180°C (200°C non-fan, gas mark 6 or equivalent)
- You will need a suitable oven dish, lightly buttered
- Combine the salmon and potatoes and transfer to the buttered dish. Make a ridged pattern on the top with a dinner fork and dot with butter. Bake for 25-30 minutes until the top is golden. Serve immediately, scattered with chopped parsley and parsley sauce (below). A few peas on the side wouldn't go amiss
- Blend the cornflour, black, white and cayenne pepper and mustard with three tablespoons of milk, taken from the measured amount in a large jug
- Heat the remaining milk in a heavy-bottomed milk pan until almost, but not actually, boiling. Stir the hot milk gradually into the cornflour mixture in the jug and whisk smooth
- Wash the pan, pour in the sauce and return to the hob to heat. Cook on a moderately high heat, whisking constantly as the mixture thickens. Add a drop more milk if it seems too thick. Check for seasoning, as you may need a little salt
- Stir in the parsley and serve immediately

SAVOURY PUDDING

CUTS INTO 16 SMALL SQUARES

Here's a tasty treat from the north of England, once enjoyed throughout Cumbria as well as Durham, Lancashire, Yorkshire and Northumberland.

Resembling a savoury flapjack, it's just the thing to keep out the cold and make the meat go further (or replace it altogether). Much like a Yorkshire pudding with beef, this was served with plenty of gravy to accompany pork, goose and duck.

It's also good with roast chicken and cold cuts from the Christmas turkey, or eaten warm or cold as a savoury snack.

Recipes vary across the region, comprising some, or all, of the following ingredients: stale bread, oats or oatmeal, onion, suet, herbs and seasoning, bound together with milk and beaten egg. It's traditional to bake it in a square tin and serve it cut into squares.

- 300ml milk
- 150g stale bread, wholemeal works well
- 110g porridge oats
- 1 medium onion, finely chopped
- Handful of spring onion tops, sliced (optional)
- 50g shredded suet (use vegetarian if you prefer)
- ½ teaspoon each of dried sage, thyme and marjoram
- Freshly ground black, and ground white, pepper
- 1 large egg
- Butter or oil for greasing (or use traditional dripping, lard or bacon fat)

- Preheat fan oven to 180°C (200°C non-fan, gas mark 6 or equivalent)
- You will need a greased rectangular tin or roasting dish, approximately 18cm square
- Heat the milk until almost boiling. Tear the bread into small pieces in a roomy bowl and pour the milk over
- Stir in the oats, onion and spring onion tops, suet, herbs and pepper. Taste and adjust the seasoning: you may want a touch of salt
- Incorporate the egg, beating quite vigorously with a wooden spoon
- Pour into the dish, smooth the top with the back of a wet metal spoon and bake for 45 minutes to 1 hour, until golden. Cut into squares and serve immediately
- It's been said no two puddings ever turn out exactly alike, not least because you can vary the herbs throughout the seasons: add a few nettle tops in the spring, and/or sweet dock shoots (bistort), fresh parsley, chives, young blackcurrant leaves and so on
- As with dock pudding, you can also serve savoury pudding for breakfast with bacon and eggs

TATIE PASTY

SERVES 6

This traditional Lakeland dish is a tasty pie and mash all in one! All you need to accompany it is a bowl of mushy peas or other vegetable of your choice. A jug of gravy wouldn't go amiss either.

Filling

- Leftover mashed potato or freshly made potato to layer the top and bottom of the pie. Approximately 600g of potatoes, before peeling and cooking

Plus

- 100g diced bacon
- 1-2 tablespoons oil
- 1 medium onion, diced
- 450-500g minced beef
- 2 rounded teaspoons black treacle
- 2 tablespoons malt or balsamic vinegar
- 1 beef gel stock pot or similar
- 8-9 tablespoons hot water (add gradually)
- Freshly ground black and ground white pepper
- Pinch of dried thyme

Pastry

- 400g plain flour
- 200g cold salted butter, diced
- 3½-4 tablespoons icy cold water

- Preheat fan oven to 180°C (200°C non-fan, gas mark 6 or equivalent)
- You will need a greased 20cm square baking tin or dish, or similar capacity round one
- Fry the bacon in a little oil until almost crispy. Remove from the pan and set aside. Fry the onion slowly, adding the remaining oil to the pan, until soft but not coloured. Add the mince and brown. Once brown, add the remaining filling ingredients and continue to cook over a medium heat for 30-40 minutes until reduced and thickened
- Make the pastry in the usual way or for speedy, extra-light results, whiz the flour and butter into fine crumbs in a food processor. Add the water and whiz until large clumps form. Remove from the machine and knead gently into a ball
- Remove a third for the lid and roll out the rest to form the body of the pie. Trim and pinch the edges, making sure they don't overhang the dish, as this makes it difficult to slice and serve the pie later
- Spread around two thirds of the mashed potatoes over the bottom of the pie (if they are cold, warm them slightly for easier spreading)
- Spoon in the filling and spread the remaining potatoes over the top
- Roll out the lid and lay it over the top, pinching it together with the sides to form a seal
- Bake for about 30-40 minutes or until piping hot and golden brown

TIP

If you're pushing the boat out, try adding a few finely chopped mushrooms and/or celery, including the green leaves, to the mince.

TRADITIONAL CHEESE AND ONION PIE

SERVES 4

Here's a favourite old cheese and onion pie recipe, popular in Cumbria.

A mature cheddar works well, but use up a mixture of odds and ends if you have bits of cheese leftover — this is an economical recipe after all. Crumbly Lancashire from across the border also works well.

Filling

- 2 large onions, fairly thinly sliced
- Cold water to almost, but not quite, cover
- 125g grated mature cheddar cheese
- Freshly ground black and ground cayenne pepper to taste
- Couple of pinches of mustard powder

Pastry

- 220g plain flour
- 110g cold salted butter, diced
- 3½ tablespoons cold water
- A little milk for finishing (or use a small egg beaten with a teaspoon of water)

- Preheat fan oven to 200°C (220°C non-fan, gas mark 7 or equivalent)
- You will need a 24cm pie dish or similar
- Simmer the onions gently in water, barely covering, for about 30 minutes until soft: pop on a lid for most of the time, removing it for the last few minutes to drive off any remaining liquid
- Transfer to a colander and leave to cool
- Make the pastry in the usual way, or for speedy extra-light results, whiz the flour and butter into fine crumbs in a food processor. Add the water and whiz until large clumps form. Remove from the machine and knead gently into a ball
- Divide the pastry in half and use half to line the bottom of the dish: roll it out a little thinner than a one-pound coin, it shouldn't be too thick. Leave a little overhang
- Arrange half the onion slices over the pastry bottom, season with the pepper and mustard and then scatter over half the cheese and repeat
- Roll out the remaining pastry and lay it carefully on top of the pie
- Pinch the lid and bottom gently together, trimming any overhang, and indent the edges. Make a steam hole in the lid. Use any leftover pastry to cut out decorative shapes
- Brush all over sparingly with milk or egg wash. Position the shapes and brush them with milk or egg wash
- Bake for 10 minutes at 200°C fan oven, then turn the oven down to 180°C fan oven (200°C non-fan, gas mark 6 or equivalent) for a further 20-25 minutes until golden
- If you have a microwave which incorporates a convection oven setting, you can use it to bake your pie. It's much more economical than your standard oven

TIPS

Use a mesh tea strainer to scatter the mustard powder over evenly, pushing it through with a teaspoon.

Fry the onions gently in a little oil if you prefer, although cooking them in water is the traditional method here.

WARMING WINTER ROOTS BAKE

SERVES 4-8

Here's a new Cumbrian recipe, very much in the spirit of traditional hearty Cumbrian meat and potato dishes. The sweet and mellow flavours of swede and parsnip really sing out in this beautiful vegetable bake — just the thing to come home to on a cold winter's day.

- 200g swede
- 200g parsnips
- 200-300g carrots
- 400g potatoes
- 1 large sprig rosemary

Plus

- 1 large onion, diced
- 1 teaspoon each butter and oil
- 2 cloves garlic, finely chopped
- 40-50g plain flour
- ½ teaspoon mustard powder
- Black, white and cayenne pepper to taste
- 300ml milk
- 75g mature cheddar cheese

Topping

- Approximately 60g dry breadcrumbs
- Another 25g grated mature cheddar cheese
- Leaves stripped from 1-2 small sprigs thyme

- Preheat fan oven to 180°C (200°C non-fan, gas mark 6 or equivalent). You will need a greased baking dish
- Peel and cut the swede, parsnips, carrots and potatoes into chunks
- Put in a pan, with cold water to cover, and add the rosemary sprig, bring to the boil and continue boiling for about 15 minutes or until tender. Drain and discard the rosemary, reserving the cooking water, and transfer to the prepared dish
- Cook the onions slowly and gently in the butter and oil over a medium heat until soft and golden, adding the garlic towards the end. Stir in the flour, mustard powder and different types of pepper and cook for 2-3 minutes, stirring constantly. Gradually add 200ml of cooking water from the vegetables, stirring until smooth. Gradually stir in the milk, turn up the heat and cook, still stirring, for another 2-3 minutes until bubbling, smooth and thickened
- Stir in the cheese and pour over the vegetables
- Combine the crumbs, extra cheese and thyme leaves and scatter evenly over the top
- Bake for 25-30 minutes until brown and bubbling. Decorate with fresh thyme sprigs to serve

WESTMORLAND LOVAGE SOUP

SERVES 3-4

You never know which way the weather's going to turn, but this lovely old-fashioned soup, based on an original Westmorland recipe, is perfect hot or chilled.

Soothing yet invigorating, it's creamy but with no need for cream. Adjust the lovage quantities to taste: as a guide, it tastes twice as strong as celery.

A valued member of many an old-fashioned Lakeland herb garden (it loves the moist local conditions and makes itself right at home), lovage is a bit of a one-off, and the sole species in its particular family. Aromatic and slightly medicinal, its strong distinctive flavour combines hints of celery, parsley and angelica.

- 1kg potatoes, peeled and diced
- 3-4 young lovage stalks
- 1 tablespoon each butter and oil
- 1 large onion, diced
- 3-4 spring onions, sliced
- 1 garlic clove, finely chopped
- 1 gel vegetable stock pot (or favourite stock cube)
- Freshly ground black and ground white pepper
- Small handful young lovage leaves, chopped

- Bring the potatoes to boil in a pan with water to cover and simmer with the lovage stalks until tender. Drain, reserving the cooking water. Discard the lovage stalks
- Heat the butter and oil in a deep pan. Fry the onions slowly until soft: add the garlic towards the end of the cooking time. Stir in the gel stock pot or crumbled cube
- Stir in the drained potatoes. Season and add the lovage leaves
- Transfer to a blender or food processor with a little cooking liquid and process until smooth. Add more liquid as necessary. Return to the pan and simmer for 5-10 minutes

TIP

Feeling a bit hot in the foot department? Pop lovage leaves in your garden wellies or walking boots. In ancient times, weary travellers slipped deodorising lovage leaves into their shoes to keep them cool and comfortable.

In common with many herbs, avoid during pregnancy or if you have any kidney problems.

WESTMORLAND TATIE POT

SERVES 4

Originally from the old Lakeland county of Westmorland, this tasty dish is as popular today as it always has been. There are many modern variations: this version is based on an old family recipe from Ambleside collected by renowned north country writer, Joan Poulson, in the 1970s.

The flavours of the lamb and black pudding complement each other beautifully and very little seasoning is required.

Source Herdwick mutton or lamb if you can and choose a beautifully seasoned crumbly black pudding with minimal visible fat.

Quantities are approximate and easy to double.

- 1 large onion, sliced or diced
- 2 tablespoons oil
- 400-500g diced mutton or lamb, trimmed of any excess fat
- 1 level tablespoon of flour
- 2 large potatoes, peeled and thinly sliced
- Freshly ground black and ground white pepper
- 100-125g black pudding
- 400ml stock (ideally beef)
- A few thyme leaves, plus extra to garnish

- Preheat fan oven to 150°C (170°C non-fan, gas mark 3 or equivalent)
- You will need a greased, lidded casserole dish (or deep oven dish with a foil 'hat')
- Fry the onions slowly in the oil until soft and golden. Remove from the pan with a slotted spoon and set aside
- Toss the lamb in the flour and brown in the pan: turn up the heat a little
- Starting and finishing with potatoes, layer the potatoes, lamb and onions, crumbling in the black pudding as you go and seasoning with both peppers and thyme leaves throughout
- Pour over the stock
- Cover and bake for 1½ hours. Remove the lid or foil and bake for the last 20 minutes or until the potatoes are golden
- Garnish with fresh thyme leaves and serve immediately with crusty bread and pickled red cabbage: mushy peas on the side work well too

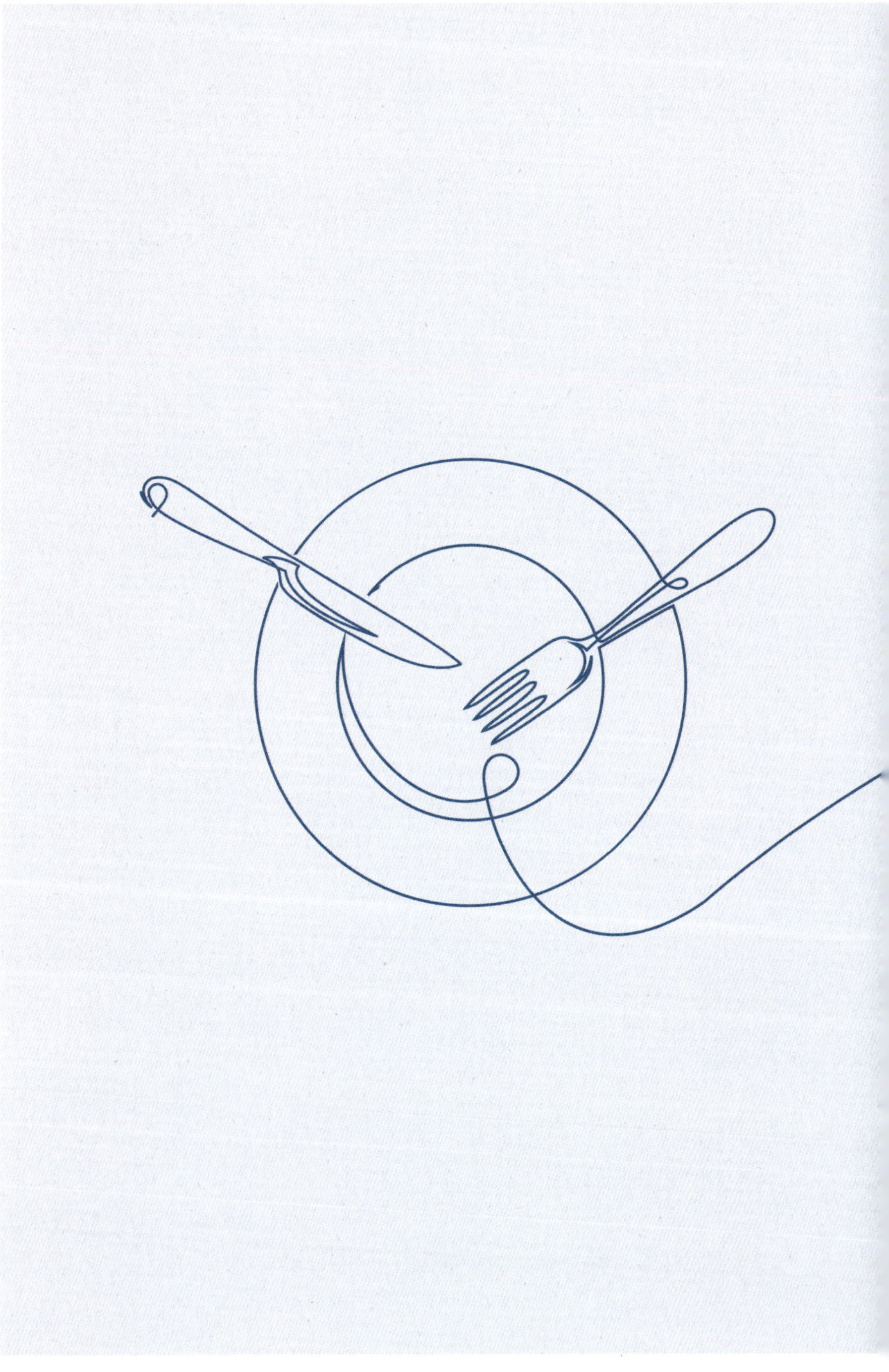

Sweet

BORDER TARTS

MAKES 12

These festive tarts come from the Scottish borders but are frequently seen in Lakeland bakers' shops. Akin to mince pies, but in tart form and therefore with half the pastry, they are handy if you're trying not to overdo it after Christmas. The filling isn't mincemeat, but a similar fruity mix with a lovely hint of butterscotch, perfect for Hogmanay or Burns Night, with a cup of tea or a seasonal sherry.

Very similar, if not identical, to Ecclefechan tarts and not dissimilar to Eyemouth tarts, all three are usually made as one large tart, but these border tarts are mini versions and there's no need to pre-bake the pastry cases as they are small enough for everything to bake together.

Pastry

- 160g plain flour
- 80g cold salted butter, diced
- 2½ tablespoons cold water

Filling

- 50g salted butter, diced
- 50g soft dark brown sugar
- 110g mixed dried fruit and peel
- 15g blanched almonds, chopped
- 1 small egg, beaten
- 25g glacé cherries, chopped

- Preheat fan oven to 180°C (200°C non-fan, gas mark 6 or equivalent)
- You will need a twelve-cup bun tin (this is a little larger than a tart tin and shallower than a muffin tin) and a 6cm (2½ inch) fluted cutter
- You can make the plain shortcrust quickly and easily in a food processor, but make it by hand if you prefer
- Whiz the flour, salt and butter into fine crumbs in the processor. Add the water and whiz again. Once it starts to form big crumbs and clump together, turn out onto a lightly floured board and form gently into a ball
- Roll the pastry gently with a lightly floured rolling pin on a lightly floured board to the thickness of just less than a pound coin. Cut into rounds and press them gently into the bun tin
- Melt the butter and sugar over a low heat in a heavy-bottomed pan. Remove from the heat. Stir in the fruit, almonds, egg and cherries and divide between the pastry cases
- Make sure all the fruit is submerged below the surface of the mixture
- Bake for 12-15 minutes until the pastry is golden and the filling has risen and is just beginning to bubble: be careful not to over-bake
- Serve warm (not hot, you'll have the roof of your mouth off!) or cold
- You can drizzle with a little glacé icing, made up with lemon juice if you like, but they are lovely as they are. Some people add a little sugar to the pastry, but it's not really needed as the filling is quite sweet and it's nice to have the plain contrast

CARAMEL APPLE GRANNY TARTS

MAKES 10 TARTS

Many caramel apple granny recipes are pie or tart-like, but some are much lighter, like a cheesecake or custard. The base might be pastry or crushed biscuits, but whatever the consistency, layers of caramel and apple are always a happy combination.

This version combines crisp, buttery pastry with a layer of salted caramel, topped with a moist apple cake. Equally lovely warm or cold.

NOTE

You need a muffin tin, rather than a tart tin, for the extra depth.
If you have no 10cm cutter, a 10cm individual fluted tart tin can be used instead to cut out the circles.

Pastry

- 200g plain flour
- 100g cold salted butter, diced
- 25g golden caster sugar
- 3 tablespoons icy-cold water

Apple topping

- 50g softened butter
- 50g golden caster sugar
- 75g plain flour
- ½ teaspoon bicarbonate of soda
- 1 level teaspoon cream of tartar
- 1 medium-large egg
- 25g ground almonds
- 110g dessert apple such as Cox's, peeled and finely diced

Caramel layer

- 10 teaspoons dulce de leche or caramel spread from a jar
- Tiny pinch of salt

- You will need a twelve-cup muffin tin, with ten cups greased, a 10cm fluted cutter and a food processor
- Preheat fan oven to 180°C (200°C non-fan, gas mark 6 or equivalent)
- The food processor makes light work of both pastry and sponge
- Whiz the flour and butter into crumbs, whiz in the sugar briefly and add the water. Pulse until large clumps form, then stop and remove the mix from the machine. Form gently into a ball by hand
- Roll out with a lightly floured rolling pin to a thickness of just less than a pound coin
- Cut out circles and transfer to the prepared tart tin, pressing the pastry circles lightly into the cups
- Whiz the butter and sugar together in the processor until pale and fluffy. Add the raising agents to the weighed flour and sieve half over the creamed mixture. Add the egg, covering with the rest of the flour, and whiz briefly. Add the almonds and apple and whiz until combined and smooth but with some apple texture remaining

Assembling the tarts

- Stir a pinch of salt into the caramel and spread a teaspoonful in the bottom of each tart. Divide the apple mixture equally between the tarts, smoothing it gently over the caramel with the back of a clean teaspoon and round the edges so the caramel won't bubble through
- Bake for about 20 minutes until the apple topping has risen, is golden and the pastry is cooked

CARAWAY BISCUITS

MAKES 20

These simple caraway biscuits were once very popular with spice-loving Cumbrians. Crumbly, buttery and delicious, they are well worth making. Tosset cakes, made over the border in Lancashire, are similar.

VARIATION Instead of sprinkling with sugar, leave them plain. This turns them into an unusual, tasty, semi-sweet biscuit to serve with cheese and celery.

Make the dough in a food processor for the best results: it's quick and easy and helps release the aromatic oils from the caraway seeds.

- 175g plain flour
- 110g salted butter, softened
- 50g caster sugar
- 1 tablespoon caraway seeds

- Preheat fan oven to 180°C (200°C non-fan, gas mark 6 or equivalent)
- You will need a 6cm fluted cutter and a baking tray lined with greaseproof paper
- Whiz the flour and butter together into fine crumbs. Add the sugar and caraway seeds and whiz until large clumps form
- Transfer the mix to an unfloured board and knead gently into a smooth — but not overworked — dough
- Cover the dough and rest in the fridge for 30 minutes
- Place on a lightly floured board and, using a rolling pin, roll to a thickness of ½cm
- Cut into rounds, sprinkle with sugar and bake for 7-8 minutes: don't over-bake, they should remain fairly pale
- Transfer to a wire rack to cool. Once completely cold, store in an airtight tin

CHOCOLATE MACAROONS

MAKES 18-20

So easy to make and so rewarding, these delicious and moreish little biscuity cakes are perfect for Christmas celebrations.

Based on the chocolate macaroons found in an old book of *Cumbria* magazine readers' recipes, this is a slightly different way of making macaroons from the usual one involving whisking up egg whites.

When you have the very chocolatey rounds on the baking tray, you think they are bound to melt all over the place, but they hold their shape surprisingly well, just spreading slightly into the usual macaroon shape.

- 125g dark chocolate, grated
- 50g golden caster sugar
- 75g ground almonds
- 1 medium egg
- ¼ teaspoon vanilla extract
- Halved glacé cherries to finish

- Preheat fan oven to 160°C (180°C non-fan, gas mark 4 or equivalent)
- You will need a baking tray, lined with greaseproof paper
- Grate the chocolate into a roomy bowl with the sugar and almonds
- Beat the egg well and add the vanilla. Stir the egg and vanilla into the chocolate, sugar and almonds
- Using two teaspoonfuls, take spoonfuls of the mixture, shaping them into round balls, and space them out on the prepared baking tray. Press half a glacé cherry into the centre of each. You may need to bake them in two batches
- Bake for 20-25 minutes: they should come away from the greaseproof paper easily and should be a little bit spongy and chewy on the inside and faintly crispy on the outside
- Transfer to a wire rack to finish cooling and once cold, store in an airtight container

TIP

It's well worth splashing out on the glamorous, deep burgundy Provencal glacé cherries for this recipe, but use the classic red ones if you prefer.

CHOCOLATE SHORTCAKE

CUTS INTO 16 SQUARES

This slightly unusual chocolate shortcake contains coconut and is adapted from a recipe from *Lakeland Cookery*, a collection of *Cumbria* magazine readers' recipes first published in 1969.

It bakes up lovely and crisp and crumbly and tastes very nice indeed. The original had a chocolate icing, but here is another one that sets the shortcake off a treat.

Originally, this recipe was printed in *Cumbria* magazine for Valentine's Day, but the sprinkles work well at any time of year.

- 125g plain flour
- 125g desiccated coconut
- 75g salted butter
- 75g dark brown sugar
- 2 level tablespoon cocoa powder

Dark chocolate covering

- 100g dark chocolate (70% cocoa) broken into pieces
- 15g salted butter, diced
- Sprinkles (optional but recommended)

- Preheat fan oven to 160°C (180°C non-fan, gas mark 4 or equivalent)
- You will need a greased 23cm brownie tin or similar, the bottom lined with greaseproof paper cut to fit
- You will need a food processor for best results
- Whiz the flour, coconut and butter together until fully combined. Add the sugar and cocoa and process well until it starts to stick slightly to the sides. Scrape down with a spatula and process briefly again
- Transfer the sandy textured crumbs to the prepared tin and press them down well: it's worth spending a little time on this. Smooth the top evenly with a wet tablespoon
- Bake for 20 minutes. The crumbs will have melded together, but it will still be fairly soft: it will crisp as it cools

Dark chocolate covering

- Melt the chocolate in the microwave in a heatproof bowl, on high, in 30 second bursts. This should take about two minutes altogether
- Alternatively, melt the chocolate in a bowl over a pan of barely simmering water: choose a bowl that will fit comfortably in the top of the saucepan without the bottom touching the hot water
- Stir the butter gently into the melted chocolate. Microwave for another 30 seconds if necessary
- Pour over the cooled, but still slightly warm, shortcake. Once the chocolate is partially set, you can mark into squares and decorate with sprinkles, if using

CLAP CAKES

MAKES 8 (EASY TO DOUBLE QUANTITIES)

Clap cakes, made from oatmeal, fat, salt and water, have been a mainstay in Cumbria for centuries. Wheat was less easy to grow in the north, but oats were much more successful and therefore a major north country grain.

Here's a lovely easy version, a little smaller and neater than the originals which would have been larger affairs shaped or 'clapped' in the hands. You'll need a food processor to grind the oatmeal a little finer and to meld the mixture together efficiently.

Light, crisp and deliciously nutty, eat with butter and/or cheese, butter and honey, jam, golden syrup or a scraping of Marmite.

And, of course, they are fabulous with generous spoonfuls of Cumberland rum butter.

- 125g oatmeal, plus an extra 2 heaped tablespoons for dusting
- ¼ teaspoon sea salt flakes
- ¼ teaspoon bicarbonate of soda
- 25g butter, melted (or lard, as originally used, if you prefer)
- 50ml hot water

- You will need a baking tray lined with greaseproof paper, a plain 7½cm round cookie-cutter and a broad palette knife
- Whiz all the oatmeal in the processor, including the extra tablespoons, until more finely textured. Remove the two tablespoons for dusting. Add the salt and bicarbonate of soda. Whiz again briefly
- Add the butter and hot water and whiz until a ball forms. Leave to stand for 10 minutes or more. (This is to allow the oatmeal to soak up all the liquid, and is an essential stage.)
- Transfer to a board. Roll in the remaining oatmeal
- Roll out ¼cm thick and cut into rounds. Keep pressing together and cut out the remainder
- Transfer to the tray using the palette knife (slip the knife under the oatcake while it's still in the cutter), leaving spaces between. Sprinkle with spare oatmeal from the board
- Bake for 20 minutes, turning carefully after about 12 minutes or until it is dry and holding together but not browned

CLIPPING TIME PUDDING

SERVES 4-6

Sheep clipping or shearing time varies around Britain, depending on the breed and the weather. Some years, further down the country, clipping time might start as early as May, but in Cumbria it's not usual to clip the famous Herdwicks much before July, and sometimes it can be later.

Many years ago, up until the Second World War, it was always a cause for celebration and ended with a clipping time supper with plenty of food, singing and dancing. The traditional pudding was known as clipping time pudding, an enriched, fruity, spicy rice pudding, sometimes so big it had to be cooked in the local baker's oven.

Make this as solid or as milky as you like. Some puddings are thick enough to slice. Some recipes give a full half pound of dried fruit to a pint of milk, making it more densely fruity, others give just a quarter of a pound. Bone marrow or suet was often used instead of butter.

Lemon zest wasn't included in original versions but gives a beautiful flavour and is highly recommended.

- 75g pudding rice (if unavailable, Arborio works well)
- Boiling water to cover
- 25-50g Demerara sugar
- ¼ teaspoon ground cinnamon and a generous grating of nutmeg
- 110g dried mixed fruit and peel
- Lightly grated zest of 1 medium lemon (avoid bitter white pith)
- 600-750ml milk (full cream milk works well)
- Knob of butter
- 1 medium egg, beaten

- Preheat fan oven to 140°C (160°C non-fan, gas mark 3 or equivalent)
- You will need a 1 litre or similar ovenproof dish, not too deep, and foil to cover
- Pour boiling water over the rice. Leave for 2 minutes and strain
- Combine the rice in the dish with 25g of the sugar, the spices, fruit and lemon zest. Pour over 600ml of the milk
- Cover with foil and bake for around 2½ hours until the rice is soft. Stir every half hour and add more milk if it seems too dry. After the first hour, test for sweetness, as you might like more sugar
- After 2 hours, remove from the oven, cool slightly and stir in the butter and beaten egg. Return to the oven and bake uncovered for the last half hour
- Serve warm or cold, on its own or with a jug of cream

COCONUT CLOUD CAKE

CUTS INTO 10 SLICES

This is such a lovely cake, soft and fluffy as a cloud. It's based on a reader's recipe sent into *Cumbria* magazine several decades ago.

If the weather is fine, you could take it out into the garden with a pot of tea, or if it's cold and wet you can console yourself with tea and cake inside.

- 175g slightly salted butter, softened
- 175g golden caster sugar
- 175g plain flour
- 1 level teaspoon bicarbonate of soda
- 2 level teaspoons cream of tartar
- 3 medium eggs, as fresh as possible, whisked
- ½ teaspoon vanilla extract (or grated zest of a lemon)
- 25g desiccated coconut
- 2 tablespoons milk

- Preheat fan oven to 160°C (180°C non-fan, gas mark 4 or equivalent)
- You will need a greased 450g loaf tin, the bottom lined with greaseproof paper
- A food processor or an electric mixer will make short work of the mixing
- Cream or whiz the butter and sugar until light and fluffy
- Combine the flour and raising agents and sieve half over the butter mixture
- Add the eggs and vanilla (or lemon), and the remaining flour and the coconut
- Whisk or whiz again. Add the milk and whisk or whiz until the mixture looks smooth and glossy
- Pour into the prepared cake tin, using a spatula to help all the mixture out
- Hollow out the centre slightly and bake in the middle of the oven for around 50 minutes, or until the cake is risen and a skewer inserted comes out clean
- Allow the cake to rest and cool down for a few moments and then carefully loosen the edges with a small palette knife: they should be starting to contract away from the sides of their own accord
- Transfer gently onto a wire rack to finish cooling
- Store in an airtight tin once cold: it's at its best fresh but will keep well for 3-4 days

TIP

The coconut adds a beautiful texture and flavour. The original recipe suggests adding either a little vanilla or lemon as well, and both are excellent. A dab of raspberry jam with your slice does no harm either: as we know, raspberries and coconut are a match made in heaven.

FIRTH STAINLESS
G DUNCAN & SON
SHEFFIELD

CUMBERLAND BRIDECAKE

CUTS INTO AT LEAST 12 SQUARES

Once upon a time, many generations ago in the Lakes, weddings were much simpler affairs, and the wedding cake, or bridecake as it was known then, was very likely a flat, currant-filled pastry. This pastry is full of Lakeland's favourite flavours: dried fruits, dark brown sugar, spices and ideally rum. It was intended to be broken into portions for the guests in a rather unusual way.

It's said that during the festivities, the bride would sit in a chair with a cloth covering her hair and the bridegroom would stand behind her holding the cake aloft. At a given signal, he would break the cake over his wife's head and the more fragments it broke into, the more children they were likely to have. Guests were encouraged to eat the broken pieces to share in the couple's luck.

Filling

- 400g mixed dried fruit and peel
- 110g butter, diced
- 50g dark brown sugar
- 5 teaspoons mixed spice
- 1 teaspoon ground ginger
- Good grating of nutmeg
- 2 tablespoons dark rum (or use orange juice)

Plus

- 320g plain flour
- 160g cold salted butter, diced
- 50g golden caster sugar
- 5 tablespoons cold water

- Preheat fan oven to 180°C (200°C non-fan, gas mark 6 or equivalent). You will need a large baking tray, lined with greaseproof paper
- Combine the filling ingredients, apart from the rum or juice, and cook over a medium heat until the sugar has melted. Stir thoroughly. Increase the heat slightly and cook for 1 minute until the liquid has slightly reduced
- Leave to cool. Stir in the rum or juice
- Rub the flour and butter into fine crumbs, stir in the sugar then add the water gradually
- A food processor makes light work of this: after adding water, pulse only until large clumps form then remove from the machine and form gently into a ball by hand
- Divide in two. Shape each into a large rectangle on a lightly floured board
- Transfer the first rectangle to the baking tray and spread with the fruit mixture
- Lay the second on top. Tuck in the edges
- Score the cake lightly into diamonds or rectangles
- Brush with water, sprinkle with caster sugar and bake for 25-30 minutes until golden
- Serve in the traditional manner or if you prefer, cut into squares and enjoy with a quiet cup of tea

CUMBERLAND COURTING CAKE

CUTS INTO 12 FINGERS

Traditional north country courting cakes are generally light and billowy affairs of sponge, piled high with cream and soft fruit, but this Cumberland courting recipe is a bit different. Outwardly more restrained, it tastes absolutely delicious: layers of pastry, apple purée and sponge are baked in a square tin, topped off with glacé icing and cut into fingers. Less showy it may be, but it is guaranteed to find favour with the apple of your eye.

Filling

- 1 medium Bramley apple, peeled, cored and chopped
- Generous squeeze of lemon juice
- 75g golden granulated sugar
- 1-2 tablespoons apple juice

Pastry

- 160g plain flour
- 80g cold salted butter, diced
- 2 tablespoons cold water

Sponge

- 50g salted butter, softened
- 50g golden caster sugar
- 1 large egg
- 50g flour
- 1 level teaspoon baking powder

- Preheat fan oven to 180°C (200°C non-fan, gas mark 6 or equivalent)
- You will need a buttered 20cm square brownie tin, the bottom lined with greaseproof paper, cut to fit
- A food processor makes short work of the pastry and sponge, but make by hand if you prefer
- Squeeze the lemon juice over the apples as you cut them and transfer to a small, heavy-bottomed saucepan. Stir in the sugar and cook gently with the apple juice until soft. Stir briskly with a wooden spoon into a rough **purée**. Cool
- For the pastry, whiz the flour and butter into crumbs in a food processor. Add the water. Whiz until large clumps form. Remove from the machine and form gently into a ball
- Roll out to the thickness of a pound coin. Line the bottom of the tin only with the pastry. Spread with the cooled purée
- For the sponge, cream the butter and sugar, beat in the egg and fold in the sieved combined flour and baking powder
- Space spoonfuls of the mixture over the purée and spread gently with a palette knife to cover the surface completely. Bake for about 20 minutes until the top has risen and it is pale golden
- Cool and ice in the tin
- For the icing, blend 225g (8oz) icing sugar with 3 tablespoons lemon juice and 1 teaspoon glycerine. Spread over the cake. A simple piped pattern in a contrasting colour icing looks pretty. Finally, cut into fingers

CUMBERLAND RUM NICKY

SERVES 8

Ideal at any time of year, but perhaps especially at Christmas, Cumberland rum nicky is probably one of the best-known Cumbrian recipes and has been around for a long time. Usually, but not always, it involves dates, ginger and rum, three of the exotic goods coming into the ports of Whitehaven, Workington and Maryport in the seventeenth century.

Rum nicky recipes vary tremendously but most often contain those three ingredients along with butter and another fruit, such as apples or dried apricots. Usually, they are pastry based but there are also cake versions.

Early pastry ones were pies with slits or 'nicks' on top to let the steam out (some say this may be the origin of the name). Later, the distinctive lattice-topped tarts became more common.

This version contains apple, but feel free to substitute soft-eating dried apricots instead. The pastry is an extra rich one.

(You should have a little pastry leftover: the generous amount is to give you some leeway when making the lattice strips.)

You could also make a pie version instead of the lattice top, if you prefer: don't forget the nicks!

Filling

- 250g cooking dates
- Water to cover
- 2 medium-sized dessert apples, peeled and cored
- 1 tablespoon lemon juice
- 2 teaspoons ground ginger
- Finely grated zest of 1 small orange
- 100g salted butter, melted
- 2 tablespoons rum
- 25g crystallised ginger

Pastry

- 250g plain flour
- 160g cold salted butter, diced
- 40g golden caster sugar
- 2-3 tablespoons icy-cold water

Plus

- A little milk for brushing over the lattice

- Preheat fan oven to 180°C (200°C non-fan, gas mark 6 or equivalent)
- You will need a greased 23cm flan dish or tin: a loose bottomed fluted one works well
- A food processor makes light work of the pastry, but make it by hand if you prefer
- Put the dates in a pan with water to cover, bring almost to the boil and simmer for 5 minutes, stirring frequently. Set aside
- Dice the apples fairly finely into a separate bowl and sprinkle with the lemon juice
- Drain the dates and add to the apples in the bowl with the orange zest and ground ginger. Stir well
- Melt the butter in a pan, add the apple mixture and rum and stir everything together. Bring almost to the boil then simmer for 5 minutes
- Leave to cool
- Tip the flour into the bowl of your food processor, add the butter and whiz into fine crumbs
- Add the sugar. Whiz briefly. Add the water and whiz again until large clumps form. Remove from the machine and knead gently into a ball with cool hands
- Divide in two. Roll out half and line the tin (the bottom shouldn't be too thick; the sides can be a little thicker)
- Roll out the remaining pastry (not too thinly this time) and cut into 10 x 2cm strips
- Ease the filling mixture into the pastry-lined tin and smooth the top. Scatter with the crystallised ginger
- Lay five strips across the tart and weave the remaining five strips across and in and out of them: you will need to fold the bottom strips gently back each time you lay another strip on top and then fold back over the next one and repeat. It's useful to watch a video online of how to do this if you've not done it before
- Press the ends of the strips and the tart edges together and brush the strips with milk
- Bake for 35-40 minutes or until golden brown

CUMBERLAND SAND CAKE

CUTS INTO 8 SLICES

Sand cake is a really old-fashioned cake you don't hear so much about now, although they still seem popular in America.

The name comes from the texture of standard flour when blended with cornflour: like fine sand, the resulting cake is lovely and light. This was sometimes recommended on cornflour packets.

Lemon is the usual flavour and rightly so, it's so delicious and fresh, but apparently, a tablespoon of rum instead of lemon zest and juice was once popular in Cumbria: now that definitely sounds worth trying!

Serve plain with a dusting of icing sugar (very good with soft fruit and maybe a little softly whipped cream, crème fraîche or Greek yoghurt), or top with a thin glacé icing made with lemon juice.

NOTE
When zesting the lemon, avoid digging into any of the white pith; it's very bitter and can spoil the flavour of your cake.

- 90g salted butter, softened
- 90g golden caster sugar
- Lightly grated zest of 1 lemon
- 75g plain flour
- 25g cornflour
- 1 level teaspoon cream of tartar
- ½ teaspoon bicarbonate of soda
- 2 medium-large eggs, beaten well with a balloon whisk
- ½ teaspoon vanilla extract
- 1 tablespoon lemon juice

- Preheat fan oven to 160°C (180°C non-fan, gas mark 4 or equivalent)
- You will need a greased 18cm cake tin
- A food processor or electric mixer will give light and speedy results
- Cream the butter, sugar and lemon zest together until light and fluffy
- Sieve the flour and cornflour together with the raising agents. Add a little to the butter mix and then the eggs, with more of the flour, and whiz briefly to combine. Add the remaining flour and whiz again. Loosen the mix with the lemon juice and whiz until smooth, but not overmixed
- Pour into the prepared tin and bake for 25 minutes until golden and a skewer inserted comes out clean
- Cool in the tin as it's a delicate cake and can easily tear while still warm

GINGER SHORTBREAD GRASMERE-STYLE

MAKES 16 SQUARES

This is adapted from an original recipe that came from the village of Sawrey, between Hawkshead and Windermere, many years ago, although it isn't clear whether it originated from Near Sawrey or Far Sawrey.

This was intended as an alternative to the secret recipe of Grasmere, and is the traditional hard biscuit-type style, rather than the softer cake style.

The poet William Wordsworth and his sister Dorothy, who lived near Grasmere from 1799-1801, were fond of gingerbread. According to Dorothy's journal, "William had a fancy for gingerbread" and once they both walked from their cottage into Grasmere, rather late in the day, to buy some.

Hard and soft shortbread was available in those days; Wordsworth was hoping for hard, but only soft was left by the time they got there. He bought it anyway, but here is a hard one he might have liked.

- 110g salted butter, softened
- 110g dark brown sugar
- 1 tablespoon golden syrup
- 225g plain flour
- 1 level teaspoon bicarbonate of soda
- 1 level teaspoon cream of tartar
- 3 teaspoons ground ginger
- 1 teaspoon mixed spice
- 2 teaspoons mixed peel
- 25g candied ginger, finely chopped

- Preheat fan oven to 140°C (160°C non-fan, gas mark 3 or equivalent)
- You will need a 20cm square brownie tin or similar, buttered and the bottom lined with greaseproof paper
- A food processor works brilliantly, but use a wooden spoon and hands if you prefer
- Whiz the butter and sugar together in the processor until creamed and fluffy. Add golden syrup and whiz to combine
- Sieve in the flour, raising agents and spices. Whiz briefly, then add the peel and candied ginger and whiz until the mixture starts to form large clumps
- Press the mixture gently into the tin. Smooth the top level with a damp metal spoon, taking time to get the surface even
- Bake for 30 minutes until the mixture is slightly pulling away from the sides of the tin
- Leave to cool in the tin, turn out and mark into squares

NOTE

Golden syrup and raising agents would be unknown to the Wordsworths, as they weren't available until the mid to late 1800s.

SHAP ROCKS

MAKES 9

These rock cakes are named after the famous pink granite excavated from Shap Quarry, near the village of Shap. Shap pink granite is a beige-pink colour, containing large pink crystals, and the darker colour particularly is prized for use in fine architecture.

The original recipe was sent into *Cumbria* magazine from a reader in the 1960s; this version is more golden-brown in colour than beige-pink, but it does contain cranberries to symbolise the crystals. They taste delicious and are perfect for a picnic.

- 225g plain flour
- 1½ teaspoons baking powder
- 110g fridge-cold salted butter, diced
- 50g golden granulated sugar
- 50g cranberries
- 2 level tablespoons redcurrant jelly, warmed slightly until runny and partially cooled
- 1 medium egg
- 3 tablespoons milk

- Preheat fan oven to 180°C (200°C non-fan, gas mark 6 or equivalent)
- You will need a large baking tray lined with greaseproof paper
- Sieve the flour and baking powder together in a roomy bowl and rub in the butter until you have fine crumbs. Stir in the sugar and cranberries. Make a well in the centre
- In a separate bowl, whisk the egg and milk together and stir in the redcurrant jelly. Stir into the dry mix
- Bring the mix together with wet hands and place on a lightly floured board. Space out nine satsuma-sized spoonfuls onto the baking tray, in rough heaps
- Bake for 12-14 minutes until golden and a skewer inserted comes out clean

TIPS

Don't overbake — you don't want actual rock cakes!

If you have an extra-sweet tooth, increase the sugar to 75g.

The original recipe suggests ringing the changes with currants or desiccated coconut, a tablespoon of caraway seeds or a teaspoon of ground ginger, all well worth trying.

SKIDDAW SHORTCAKE

CUTS INTO 16 SQUARES

It is a well-known fact that Cumbria has no end of brilliant gingerbread and gingerbread-type recipes, including both soft and hard kinds. Incidentally, the poet William Wordsworth favoured the hard variety, although he would eat soft if the hard had sold out.

Here's a light and simple harder variety, based on an old Women's Institute member's recipe and once sold at Wigton Women's Institute market by the Cumbria-Westmorland Women's Institute Market Society. It's absolutely lovely and could be just what you fancy with a cup of tea or coffee for a weekday pick-me-up.

The original was topped with a ginger buttercream icing, but a coating of melted dark chocolate works beautifully to turn the shortcake into a weekend treat.

- 175g salted butter, softened
- 75g golden granulated sugar
- 225g plain flour
- 1 level teaspoon baking powder
- 2 teaspoons ginger, or to taste

Dark chocolate covering

- 100g dark chocolate (70% cocoa) broken into pieces
- 15g salted butter, diced

- Preheat fan oven to 160°C (180°C non-fan, gas mark 4 or equivalent)
- You will need a 23cm brownie tin or similar, the bottom lined with greaseproof paper cut to fit
- Cream the butter and sugar until light and fluffy by hand or whiz in a food processor
- Combine the flour, baking powder and ginger, and sieve into the butter mixture in 5-6 batches, working each batch in as you go: you can do this by hand with a wooden spoon or whiz in a food processor, again in batches
- Press into the prepared tin: this is the hardest part as the mixture is quite stiff
- Smooth the top evenly with a wet tablespoon
- Bake for about 40 minutes until golden and crisp. Cool and cut into squares in the tin

Dark chocolate covering

- This is sufficient to coat half the shortcakes, but use double quantities if you would like to coat the lot. Melt the chocolate in the microwave in a heatproof bowl, on a high heat, in 30 second bursts. This should take around two minutes altogether
- Alternatively, melt the chocolate in a bowl over a pan of barely simmering water: choose a bowl that will fit comfortably in the top of the saucepan, without the bottom touching the hot water
- Stir the butter gently into the melted chocolate. Microwave for another 30 seconds if necessary. Pour immediately over the cooled shortcake

STICKY TOFFEE PUDDING

MAKES 4-8

This modern Lakeland classic first appeared at the Sharrow Bay Country House Hotel in Ullswater during the 1970s. The village of Cartmel is also famous for its own deliciously sticky toffee puddings, which are popular nationwide.

You can make this baked version at home in your own kitchen. Full of good things, you might make it your last pre Lent treat on Shrove Tuesday instead of pancakes.

- 100g dates
- 50ml boiling water
- ½ teaspoon bicarbonate of soda

Plus

- 100g soft muscovado sugar
- 25g butter, softened
- 2 tablespoons black treacle
- 100g flour
- 1¼ teaspoons baking powder
- 1 large egg, well beaten
- 1 teaspoon vanilla extract

Sticky toffee sauce

- 75g salted butter
- 100g muscovado sugar
- 75ml double cream

- Preheat fan oven to 160°C (180°C non-fan, gas mark 4 or equivalent)
- You will need a food processor for best results
- Soften and tenderise the dates: lay them in a flat dish, add the bicarbonate of soda to the boiling water and pour over. Set aside for 30 minutes
- Whiz the sugar in the processor to eliminate any hard lumps. Add the butter and whiz until fluffy. Add the dates and soaking water, and whiz smooth. Add the treacle and whiz again
- Combine the flour and baking powder and sieve over the top. Finally, add the egg and vanilla and whiz until everything is smooth and glossy
- Once the oven comes up to temperature, set a dish of hot water on the bottom shelf
- Pour the mixture into four greased and floured dariole moulds and set on a baking tray. Alternatively, for slightly smaller puddings, grease eight cups of a 12-cup muffin tin
- Bake for 18-30 minutes depending on the chosen mould size, or until risen and a skewer inserted comes out clean. Avoid over-baking

Sticky toffee sauce

- Combine the butter, sugar and cream in a small, heavy-bottomed saucepan. Bring to the boil and simmer for 3-5 minutes until thick and smooth
- Turn out the puddings. Brush the tops and sides liberally with the sauce (or pour it over). Serve with remaining sauce, a jug of cream or custard

STICKY WIGTON GINGERBREAD

CUTS INTO 16 SQUARES

This spicy, moist and fruity gingerbread is perfect for Guy Fawkes Night, and is adapted from an original recipe from Wigton. Cumbria is famous for its gingerbread, which is only natural, as during the sixteenth century Lakeland locals were treated to plentiful supplies of exotic spices, Barbados sugar, dried fruits and rum arriving on their doorstep in the ports of Whitehaven, Workington and Maryport. These have been used extensively in Cumbrian cooking ever since.

There are two main kinds of Cumbrian gingerbread: hard and soft. The famous Grasmere gingerbread is a hard type, while this one from Wigton is most definitely soft. Try serving it with thick cream for extra deliciousness.

- 225g flour
- 2-4 teaspoons ground ginger, according to taste
- 1 teaspoon ground cinnamon
- 1 teaspoon ground mixed spice
- 2 teaspoons baking powder

Plus

- 50g dark brown sugar
- 200g salted butter, diced
- 7 rounded tablespoons golden syrup
- 110g raisins
- 1 large egg, beaten

- Preheat fan oven to 160°C (180°C non-fan, gas mark 4 or equivalent)
- You will need a lightly buttered 20cm tin, the bottom lined with greaseproof paper cut to fit
- Combine the flour, spices and baking powder in a roomy bowl and gently heat the sugar, butter and syrup together until melted and the sugar has lost its grittiness
- Stir in the raisins once the butter mix has melted and leave to cool slightly
- Sieve the dry ingredients over in batches, whisking to combine as you go. Whisk in the egg with the last couple of batches. Continue to whisk until smooth
- Pour into the tin and bake for 35-40 minutes until springy to the touch and a skewer inserted comes out clean
- Cut into squares while warm. It's lovely warm, as well as cold, and a dab of clotted cream goes very nicely with it

WESTMORLAND CREAM PANCAKES FOR SHROVETIDE

MAKES AROUND 6, DEPENDING ON PAN SIZE

Adapted from an unusual old Westmorland recipe, these pancakes contain no eggs but are still very much in keeping with the spirit of Shrove Tuesday, or Mardi Gras ('Fat Tuesday') as they say in France.

Made with half milk, half cream, they are absolutely delicious, possibly even more so than standard pancakes made with egg.

Serve as usual with lemon and sugar, syrup, honey or jam: blackcurrant is especially good.

Alternatively, you can use mincemeat or summer berries to fill the pancakes, and if there is any more cream going spare, splash some of that over as well!

- 150ml single cream
- 150ml milk
- ½ teaspoon bicarbonate of soda
- 1 level teaspoon cream of tartar
- 110g flour
- Pinch salt
- Butter for greasing

- Blend the milk and cream together in a roomy bowl and whisk in the bicarbonate of soda and cream of tartar
- Sieve in the flour gradually, whisking as you go. Add the salt and give the batter a final thorough whisking
- Pour the batter into a jug for ease
- Lightly butter a small frying pan (or a larger pan, depending on the size of your pancakes) and heat until the butter starts sizzling gently
- Pour in enough batter to coat the pan thinly (the cream batter is slightly thicker than normal) and cook for two minutes each side until golden

TIP For best results, use the batter immediately.

WESTMORLAND KINGS

SERVES 4-6

This old recipe from Lazonby in the lower Eden Valley may look a little rustic, but it tastes absolutely delicious. Very simple, it's jam-packed with apples held together by a light sponge batter. The name is a bit of a mystery: if anyone knows the story behind the name please get in touch via *Cumbria and Lakeland Walker* magazine.

Filling

- 3 medium-large Bramley apples, combined weight around 750g
- 3 tablespoons lemon juice
- 75g Demerara sugar
- 3 tablespoons apple juice (or water)

Sponge batter

- 50g plain flour
- ½ teaspoon baking powder
- 25g salted butter
- 75g Demerara sugar
- 1 medium-large egg, beaten
- 2 tablespoons milk

- Preheat fan oven to 180°C (200°C non-fan, gas mark 6 or equivalent)
- You will need a greased 1.1 litre pudding basin, string and foil to cover (plus a roasting dish if baking in the oven)
- Peel, core and slice the apples fairly thinly. Add the lemon juice to give an extra zesty flavour and to prevent browning
- Cook the apples gently with the sugar and apple juice (or water) for 5-10 minutes or until just tender. Drain off the juice and set aside, reserving the juice
- Sieve the flour and baking powder together and rub in the butter to form crumbs. Stir in the sugar and mix in the egg and milk to form a loose batter
- Mix in the apple slices and transfer to the basin
- Cover the top with a loose lid of foil, secured with string
- Either steam for 2 hours or bake for 50-60 minutes in a roasting dish half-filled with hot water, until the top is golden and a skewer inserted comes out clean
- Serve with cream or custard and the warmed reserved juice

WESTMORLAND PEPPER CAKE

CUTS INTO 8-12 SLICES

Once upon a time, pepper cake was the customary Christmas cake in the north west. Made for family and friends, it was also traditionally offered when carol singers and bands of musicians, known as Christmas Waits, came calling.

Recipes across the north and north west vary, and many have a lot in common with gingerbread. Some, like Yorkshire pepper cake, contain no fruit at all, others a modest amount. This version from Westmorland is more plentiful in the fruit department than most and has no extra sugar, other than the syrup and treacle.

There is pepper in this cake, but it's worth remembering that pepper was a general term years ago for any pungent spice.

- 150g butter
- 2 tablespoons golden syrup
- 4 tablespoons black treacle
- 250g plain flour
- 1½ teaspoons baking powder
- ¼ teaspoon ground cloves
- ¼ teaspoon ground black pepper
- 1 teaspoon ground ginger
- 1 egg, made up to 200ml with milk
- 350g mixed dried fruit and peel

- Preheat fan oven to 140°C (160°C non-fan, gas mark 3 or equivalent)
- You will need a greased 20cm cake tin or silicone mould
- Melt the butter, syrup and treacle slowly in a small pan. Stir thoroughly
- Sieve the flour, baking powder and spices into a roomy bowl that will fit comfortably into the crook of your arm
- Make a well and pour in the syrup mixture
- Using a fork, and holding the bowl under your arm, gradually draw the syrup mixture through the flour
- Once fully combined, beat the egg and milk together and add gradually to the mixture, stirring constantly, until all is incorporated
- As the mixture loosens, change to a whisk. Once smooth, stir in the fruit
- Pour into the prepared tin and bake for about 1 hour or until a skewer inserted comes out clean. Cool in the tin
- You can cut into the cake straightaway or keep it for a couple of weeks in an airtight tin to deepen in flavour and texture
- As with any northern fruit cake, a slice of cheese on the side sets it off a treat: a nice mature cheddar, or crumbly Lancashire or Wensleydale all complement the cake beautifully

WINDERMERE SPICE BISCUITS

MAKES APPROXIMATELY 15

These lovely biscuits, attributed to the Windermere area, have the most beautiful flavour and are very moreish. Caraway seeds have been used in recipes for centuries and were very popular in Georgian times. They are said to aid digestion and these certainly make a cheering treat: take it easy and enjoy them with a a restorative cup of tea.

- 110g salted butter, softened
- 75g soft light brown sugar (disperse any lumps that may have formed)
- 175g plain flour
- ½ teaspoon ground cinnamon
- ½ teaspoon ground ginger
- 1 teaspoon caraway seeds
- 1 medium-large egg, beaten

- Preheat fan oven to 180°C (200°C non-fan, gas mark 6 or equivalent)
- You will need a 6cm fluted cutter and a large baking tray, greased or lined with greaseproof paper
- Beat the butter and sugar together with a wooden spoon until light and fluffy and pale in colour
- Combine the flour, spices and caraway seeds and incorporate gradually into the butter and sugar
- Mix in the egg to make a stiff paste
- Knead gently into a smooth, workable dough
- Roll out on a lightly floured board to the thickness of a pound coin and cut into rounds
- Arrange on the baking tray and bake for about 15 minutes or until pale golden and not at all brown, and they lift easily off the tray with a palette knife
- Cool on a wire rack and store in an airtight tin

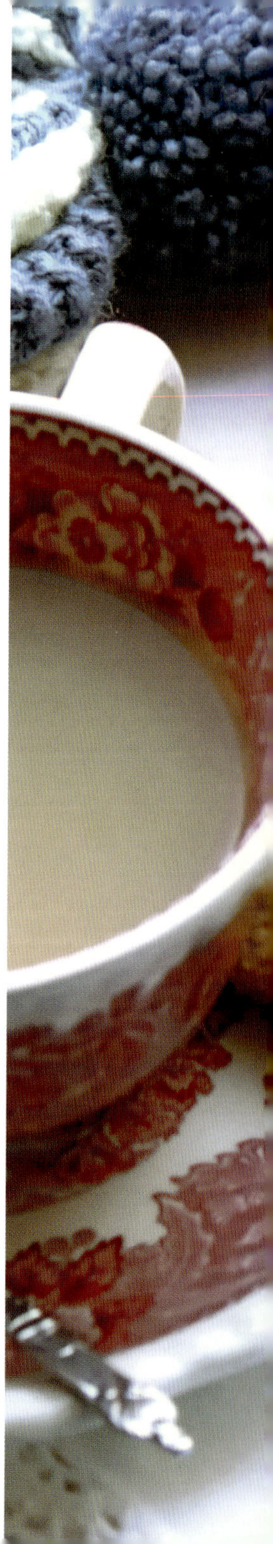

WITHERSLACK DAMSON COBBLER

SERVES 4-6

Damsons are an old variety of semi-wild plum, smaller than regular plums but larger than bullaces and sloes (the smallest of the plum family, and the only one with thorns). They have a beautiful tart, yet rich and deep flavour when cooked with sugar.

The famous Witherslack damsons, tucked away in the Lyth Valley, are said to have the best and most aromatic flavour of them all.

This light and crumbly cobbler topping provides the perfect contrast of taste and texture and sets the damsons off a treat.

It may seem counter-intuitive to squeeze the cobbles of dough into shape, but they survive this unexpected rough handling with beautifully light results.

- 800g damsons
- 75g golden caster sugar, or to taste
- 5-6 tablespoons water

Plus

- 250g plain flour
- 2 level teaspoons baking powder
- 175g golden caster sugar
- 150g salted butter, melted

- Preheat fan oven to 180°C (200°C non-fan, gas mark 6 or equivalent)
- You will need a 1 litre capacity baking dish and a baking tray
- Cook the damsons gently with the sugar and water until tender and the stones come away a little more easily. Remove the stones. See note below
- Spoon the damsons into the baking dish: it should come ¾ of the way up to the top. Set the dish on a baking tray (this will prevent any drips of juice spilling over onto the bottom of the oven)
- Combine the flour, baking powder and sugar and stir in the melted butter (you can do this in a food processor if you like)
- Working quickly, while the dough is still warm, take satsuma-sized balls of the rich, crumbly dough and squeeze and shape them into flat discs 1cm thick. Lay over the fruit, touching but not overlapping. You should have 8 or 9 'cobbles'
- Bake for about 25 minutes until the cobbles are golden and the fruit bubbling
- Sprinkle the top with extra sugar before serving with thick cream or custard

NOTE

Damsons are a clingstone type of plum, unlike the fully domesticated Victoria which is freestone and whose stones come away easily.

Also by Mrs Simkins

Traditional Yorkshire Cooking

More than 60 North Country recipes, from Cinder Toffee to Yorkshire Moggy